Foxy Foxes
2nd ed. March 13, 2015

Book design by John Wagner

Photographs by John Wagner

Also by John Wagner

First Flight, Journey of a Man and an Eagle

The Magnificent Wild Mustangs of Sand Wash Basin

**Picasso: Wild Stallion of the West
The Icon of Sand Wash Basin**

The Bird Herd of Sand Wash Basin

Fighting Stallions of Sand Wash Basin

Frightful Freefall's Photo Album

Rock Art & Ruins of Northwestern Colorado and Northeastern Utah

Foxy Foxes

By

John A. Wagner

"I wonder where my brother is."

"Brother, why are you snarling at me?"

"Did you hid my favorite fur toy."

"I didn't take your fur toy."

"I can smell it on you!"

"Don't push me, brother!"

"Take that back!"

"I'm telling Dad!"

"I'm telling Mom!"

![Two foxes playing]

"Copy Cat!"

"I'm not either!"

"Last time, you take that back!"

"I take it back, Big Brother."

"What's that strange buzzing sound?"

"I see it!"

"I'm going to catch that Buzzing Bug!"

"Almost caught it this time."

"There it is!"

"You can't get away from me!"

"Blast, I almost had it!"

"Bye, Buzzing Bug. I'll catch you next time!"

"Ha-ha! Nobody will see me here."

"What is Rudi doing?"

"Wow, a monster rock that needs to be conquered."
said Rudi.

"One slip and I will fall zillions of feet!"

"Woohoo! I did it!"

Full of Curiosity.

I need a swamp cooler!

"Why does my tongue pop-out, when I stretch?"

I hope Big Brother doesn't see me with the Fur Toy!

Somebody gave me fleas. Brother!

Why does Rudi, the runt, get blamed for everything?

My Rock Collection.

I hope you have enjoyed the book "Foxy Foxes."
It was a fun book to make.

Here's a little information on a red fox.

Red Fox

Weight: 12-16 pounds.

Tail: 15-17 inches long.

Head & Body: 23-26 inches long.

Color: Reddish-yellow, with a white belly. Bushy tail tipped with white…Note: Not all Red Foxes are red! There is 4 different color phases of the Red Fox such as black, cross, silver and red. But in all, the color phases the tail is always white-tipped.

The young are born in March or April.

Gestation time: 51-52 days.

One litter per year: 4-9 pups per litter.

The pups or kits remain in their den for at least a month.

The pups are very playful and curious. They are fun to photograph. You never know what they will do next.

John A Wagner lives in the little town of Dinosaur, Colorado with his wife Sarah, daughter Megan & their dog Buddy.

One of John's favorite pastimes is photographing the wild horses of Sand Wash Basin.

As John says, "Heaven to the Cowboy was spending time on the open range where he could talk to God in his own way."

www.ingramcontent.com/pod-product-compliance
Lightning Source LLC
Chambersburg PA
CBHW041522280526
45792CB00004B/1343